W9-CKF-985

PRINCE

PRINCE

THE MAN, THE SYMBOL, THE MUSIC

Eric Braun

LERNER PUBLICATIONS ◆ MINNEAPOLIS

Copyright © 2017 by Lerner Publishing Group, Inc.

All rights reserved. International copyright secured. No part of this book may be reproduced, stored in a retrieval system, or transmitted in any form or by any means—electronic, mechanical, photocopying, recording, or otherwise—without the prior written permission of Lerner Publishing Group, Inc., except for the inclusion of brief quotations in an acknowledged review.

Lerner Publications Company
A division of Lerner Publishing Group, Inc.
241 First Avenue North
Minneapolis, MN USA 55401

For reading levels and more information, look up this title at www.lernerbooks.com.

The images in this book are used with the permission of: © The Life Picture Collection/Getty Images, p. 2; © Kevin Kane/WireImage/Getty Images, pp. 6, 10; © Jeff Kravitz/FilmMagic/Getty Images, p. 8; © Frank Micelotta/Getty Images, p. 9; © Tim Mosenfelder/Getty Images, p. 12; © Mark Ralston/AFP/Getty Images, p. 13; © Jim Steinfeldt/Michael Ochs Archives/Getty Images, p. 14; Seth Poppel Yearbook Library, pp. 16, 17, 18; © Afro American Newspapers/Gado/Getty Images, p. 20; © Rayn Barnett/Michael Ochs Archives/Getty Images, p. 21; AP Photo/Charles Borst, p. 23; © Robert Matheu/Camera Press/Redux, p. 24; © Waring Abbott/Getty Images, p. 25; © Ebt Roberts/Redferns/Getty Images, p. 26; © DWD-Media /Alamy, p. 27; © Bettmann/Getty Images, p. 28; © Everett Collection/Warner Bros. Pictures/Alamy, p. 31; © Richard E. Aarons/Redferns/Getty Images, p. 32; Carlos Gonzalez/Collection/Newscom, p. 33; © Rob Verhorst/Redferns/Getty Images, p. 35; © Kevin Mazur/Getty Images, p. 37; AP Photo/Chris O'Meara, p. 39; © Lester Cohen/WireImage/Getty Images, p. 40.

Front cover: Marilyn Kingwill/Landmark Media/Newscom.

Main body text set in Rotis Serif Std 55 Regular 13.5/17. Typeface provided by Adobe Systems.

Library of Congress Cataloging-in-Publication Data

Names: Braun, Eric, 1971– author.
Title: Prince : the man, the symbol, the music / Eric Braun.
Description: Minneapolis : Lerner Publications, 2017. | Series: Gateway biographies | Includes bibliographical references and index.
Identifiers: LCCN 2016026942 (print) | LCCN 2016028073 (ebook) | ISBN 9781512434569 (lb : alk. paper) | ISBN 9781512434576 (eb pdf)
Subjects: LCSH: Prince—Juvenile literature. | Rock musicians—Biography—Juvenile literature.
Classification: LCC ML3930.P756 B73 2017 (print) | LCC ML3930.P756 (ebook) | DDC 781.66092 [B] —dc23

LC record available at https://lccn.loc.gov/2016026942

Manufactured in the United States of America
1-42106-25399-9/13/2016

CONTENTS

A Childhood in Music   14

Creating a Controversy   19

Purple Rain   24

Fighting for Control   32

Going It Alone   37

Important Dates   42
Source Notes   44
Selected Bibliography   45
Further Reading   47
Index   48

Prince speaks at his induction into the Rock & Roll Hall of Fame in 2004.

At first, you hardly knew he was there.

The stage at the Rock & Roll Hall of Fame induction ceremony that night in 2004 was crowded with musicians. But Prince, one of the biggest pop stars of the 1980s, stood off to the side, almost in the dark. At one point in 1984, he'd had the number one single, the number one album, and the number one movie in the United States. Yet he seemed somewhat out of place with the classic rock stars, including Tom Petty and Steve Winwood. Dressed in a black suit with a bright red shirt and hat instead of his customary purple, Prince strummed his guitar and seemed content to blend into the background.

Many musicians and music journalists considered Prince a genius. He was an expert at dozens of different instruments, and he was among the best guitar players alive. He wrote beautiful, super-catchy songs with lyrics that were intelligent, poetic, romantic, and often shocking. Over a career of nearly three decades, he had written dozens of massive hits for himself as well as for others. Prince had spent his career bringing together the world of black music and the world of traditional rock music, which was mostly made by white people. For these reasons, Prince was also inducted into the Rock Hall that night.

But this performance was not about him. The musicians were gathered to celebrate the induction of legendary Beatles guitarist George Harrison, who had died in 2001, into the Rock Hall. They were playing one of Harrison's most famous songs, "While My Guitar Gently Weeps." Harrison's son, Dhani, was also onstage playing guitar.

A group of rock stars plays a tribute to Beatles guitarist George Harrison at the 19th annual Rock & Roll Hall of Fame induction ceremony.

The band began by playing the song much like it sounds on the Beatles' self-titled album, where it first appeared in 1968. Then, near the end, the tone of the performance changed. First, Dhani looked toward the side of the stage and broke into a smile. Next, we heard the first familiar note of the song's final guitar solo. It seemed to erupt from that dark corner where Prince had been standing. Prince moved toward the center of the stage. A spotlight picked him up.

Within seconds, Prince began to expand the sound. He picked and bent notes to create something that simultaneously sounded fresh and exciting but also recognizable as the famous solo.

Prince surprises the audience with a wildly impressive solo at the 2004 Rock & Roll Hall of Fame induction ceremony. Dhani Harrison plays guitar in the background.

As Prince's playing became more complicated and impressive, he opened his mouth. He shut his eyes. He shook his head as if even he couldn't believe how great it sounded. Tom Petty nodded in approval. "I remember I leaned out at him at one point and gave him a 'This is going great!' kind of look," Petty recalled later. "He just burned it up. You could feel the electricity of 'something really big's going down here.'"

Prince then turned his back to the audience and gave the other performers a look as if to let them know he wasn't finished. Dhani Harrison, who seemed to be having the time of his life, again lit up with a huge smile as

Prince plays his own set at the 2004 Rock & Roll Hall of Fame party.

Prince fell backward into the crowd. Someone caught him and lifted him back onstage—all while Prince kept playing guitar. Petty kept singing.

The song began to wind down, and Prince bent the final notes of the solo—more recognizable as the final bars of Harrison's masterpiece. Finally, as the drummer bashed his cymbals for the big finish, Prince lifted his guitar off his neck and threw it straight up into the air. Then he turned and walked off the stage. His steps had a bounce of confidence and pride. The guitar never came down.

Rock critics loved his performance. So did casual fans. Many years later, when Prince died unexpectedly, it was this moment that many people remembered first.

Prince's induction into the Rock & Roll Hall of Fame that night was an important part of his legacy. It meant that he had joined the ranks of the greatest rock stars of all time. But most people expected he would end up there someday, given his record sales and stature in the music world. His performance on "While My Guitar Gently Weeps" may have been more important than actually getting into the Rock Hall.

For years Prince had been known as an eccentric. He'd worked alone in his studio to make the music he wanted to make. He'd thrown curveballs at the recording industry and his fans. He'd gone to war with his record label over the rights to his music, which probably cost him record sales. He was quiet and reclusive, visiting his local church

Prince performs in 1997. His persona and style were always beyond the mainstream.

and riding his bicycle around his neighborhood. He didn't fit cleanly into the mold of a huge pop icon. As Prince soloed that night, all the things that made him a great artist came alive for everyone to see: his amazing skill on the guitar, his flamboyance as a performer, and his unique style that made him a musical genre unto himself.

After his unexpected death in April 2016, fans visited his home and studio outside of Minneapolis, leaving notes, flowers, and remembrances. One quote that seemed to appear more than any other was the title of a famous song Prince had written for another artist: "Nothing Compares 2 U." On the night of the Rock Hall ceremony, the world was reminded of what an incomparable talent he was. He wasn't just a rock star, a pop star, an R&B star, a black artist, or a great guitar player. He was Prince. And the world of music has never seen anyone quite like him before or since.

A Prince fan pays her respects outside Prince's Paisley Park home and studio near Minneapolis after his death in 2016.

A Childhood in Music

Prince Rogers Nelson was born on June 7, 1958, into a family of musicians, and his very name meant music. His mother, Mattie Shaw, had been a singer in a jazz band called the Prince Rogers Trio. His father, John Nelson, was a pianist and the leader of that band. Prince Rogers was his stage name. The couple gave their son the band's name.

From an early age, Prince was tuned into music. His mother said that when he was three years old, he would slip away from her in department stores to find the musical instruments. He would play the piano, the organ, or any instrument he could find in the store. "I'd have to hunt for him," his mother said, "and that's where he'd be—in the music department."

Young Prince heard a lot of music in his home.

John Nelson accepts a Minnesota Music Award on behalf of his son Prince for the song "Kiss" in 1987.

He also heard it at church. His parents were Seventh-day Adventists (SDAs) and took him to church regularly. Prince once told an interviewer that the main thing he got out of church was the choir music.

Something else Prince heard a lot of was his parents arguing. When Prince was seven years old, they separated, and he lived with his mom. The separation was very painful for Prince, especially when his mother began dating another man. She married Hayward Baker in 1967, and he and Prince disliked each other right away. Before long, because of his fighting with Baker, Prince left his mother's home to live with his dad. When Prince was older, he hinted that Baker had been violent and abusive.

By the time he moved in with his dad, Prince had taken a few piano and guitar lessons, but he was not a good student. He didn't want to play the songs that teachers tried to teach him. When he played his own songs, he was criticized. So he stopped taking lessons and continued to teach himself.

The music he listened to varied widely, from funk, R&B, and the blues to classic rock and classical and more. He also played a wide variety of instruments. In junior high, he was in the band that backed up the school choir. Prince was the keyboardist, but he could play the guitar and drums better than the guitarist and drummer.

While music came easily to Prince, his home life was still hard. He moved out of his dad's home to stay with an aunt, but then he returned to live with his dad. For a while, he lived in a foster home. He later recalled, "I didn't like being shuffled around. I was a bitter kid for a while, but I adjusted."

Prince lived for a time in the basement of his friend André's house. André's mom, Bernadette, treated him well and supported his love of music. Prince and André stayed up late, listening to and making music.

Kids at school often picked on Prince. He was the shortest kid in his class by a lot, and the other black kids thought his skin was too light. The rejection at school added to the rejection he felt from his mom and dad, and it seemed to drive him to work harder at his music, perhaps as a way to prove to himself and others that he had value. It also made him shy and awkward socially. He

had a hard time making friends. He was a very good basketball player, but he didn't start for his school team because of his size. He ate lunch alone every day.

Meanwhile, he was already making a name for himself as a musician.

Prince's eighth-grade yearbook photo from 1972

16

Prince *(far right)*
in eighth grade
with two of
his basketball
teammates

At the age of
thirteen, Prince
was playing in a
band called Grand
Central in various
clubs around
Minneapolis. Though he was barely a teenager, word of
his talent began to spread around town. People came to
Grand Central shows specifically to see the skinny kid
with the huge Afro play.

Prince dreamt of becoming a massive rock star, and
that meant hard work. In high school, he spent countless
hours in the school music room, playing piano, guitar,
and other instruments. Long after the rest of the students
had gone home, he practiced alone in the room. He not
only mastered many instruments, but he also taught
himself to write music. And besides the regular music
classes he took at school, he also took a class on the
business of music. He wanted to learn everything he
could about the professional side of being a musician. The
class covered contracts, copyrights, and more.

Prince soon attracted the attention of a concert promoter named Owen Husney. To convince Prince to hire him as his manager, Husney raised $50,000 to support the young musician while he worked on a demo they could send to major record companies. When they sent out the finished demo, they got at least three offers. Prince turned down offers from A&M and Columbia, because they wouldn't give him complete creative control. Warner Bros. offered complete artistic freedom and agreed to let him produce the albums. But first, they wanted to see him in action.

Warner Bros. executives went into the studio with Prince while he recorded a song. First, he recorded the

guitar track. Then he recorded the drums. According to one Warner Bros. vice president, they knew at that point that Prince was a major talent. They told him that he didn't need to finish. They had seen enough. But Prince was determined to complete the song, so he did all the other tracks.

Prince in 1974, during his sophomore year at Central High School

Afterward, Prince told the Warner Bros. executives, "Don't make me black." At that time, black and white artists were marketed and sold in distinct ways. Black artists were played on R&B radio stations and mostly attracted black audiences, while white artists were played on pop stations and mostly attracted white audiences. Prince was saying that he was a musician in a much bigger sense. He could make music for everyone. He also knew that if he was marketed only to black audiences, he could never be the rock star he dreamed of being. He needed to reach a bigger audience. The executives were blown away by his talent but also by his knowledge and confidence.

Warner Bros. signed Prince to a three-record deal. Not only did the contract give him creative control and the right to produce his own albums, but it also promised to market him as a pop artist, not as an R&B artist. The contract was rumored to pay him more than $1 million. Prince was nineteen years old.

Creating a Controversy

Prince went to Sausalito, California, to begin recording his first album, *For You*. As his contract stipulated, he played all the instruments. He might start by recording the drum part, followed by the guitar part, then the keyboard, and so on. Vocals usually came last. When he was finished, all the separate tracks were combined to make a song. In all, Prince played twenty-seven different instruments on the album.

Reviews of the 1978 album were mixed. The album showed promise, critics said, and Prince was clearly talented. But it wasn't a great album.

Nevertheless, it was time for Prince to put together a band so he could go on tour to support the record. He recruited musicians he knew from Minnesota, starting with his friend André. Prince made a point of composing his band of black, white, male, and female members. He wanted to break down barriers.

André Cymone (*pictured*) spent many hours playing music with Prince when both artists were young. Cymone later had his own solo career.

They played a couple of shows at a theater in north Minneapolis, and executives from Warner Bros. flew in to watch one of them. At that time, Prince was still figuring out what his act would be like onstage. The show didn't go very well, and Warner Bros. decided that Prince should not tour after all. Instead, he should work on his second album—and practice his live act.

So Prince went back to the studio. The record, *Prince*, contained a song that would become his first big hit, "I Wanna Be Your Lover." The song made it to number 11 on the pop charts.

Meanwhile, the band practiced hard. As keyboardist Matt Fink later remembered, "We rehearsed like crazy for many months." When they were offered the chance to perform on *American Bandstand*, a popular rock-and-roll TV show, they were ready.

Prince toured as the opening act for Rick James, a successful R&B performer. James agreed to put Prince on the tour, but he disliked Prince. He publicly criticized

Prince's determination to be marketed to a pop audience, saying, "He doesn't want to be black."

A nineteen-year-old Prince performs at the Roxy Theatre in Los Angeles in 1979.

Yet Prince was wise to insist on going pop. At that time, R&B artists were having very little mainstream success. The crossover appeal was working too. The album *Prince* sold more than a million copies. Prince's third album, which he recorded on his own in Minneapolis, more clearly blended genres than his first two. Titled *Dirty Mind*, the record had funk, soul, rock, and dance jams. It also had Prince's first blockbuster hit, "When You Were Mine," an organ-driven new wave pop song. The album earned Prince a story in *Rolling Stone*, the most influential pop music magazine, and an appearance on the TV show *Saturday Night Live*.

While critics loved *Dirty Mind*, it didn't sell very well. The album got as much attention for its sexual lyrics and the photo of a nearly nude Prince on the cover as it did for its music. The explicit content kept it off the radio, and since it didn't fit neatly into any category, it confused fans. Matt Fink summed up the reaction to *Dirty Mind*: "It was so innovative and different, it threw people for a loop."

Prince learned just how much he'd thrown his fans for a loop when the Rolling Stones invited him to tour with them in 1981. Prince loved the Stones, one of the greatest rock-and-roll bands of all time, and surely was flattered with the invitation to open for them. The Stones's lead singer Mick Jagger and guitarist Keith Richards also loved Prince and wanted to expose him to a bigger audience.

In their first show, Prince came out in his outrageous

The Rolling Stones play a venue in Illinois on their 1981 tour. This show drew a crowd of nine thousand fans.

stage outfit—bikini underwear, thigh-high stockings, high-heeled boots, and a trench coat. And when the band began to play its genre-warping music, the confused rock fans began to boo, make obscene gestures, and throw food and soda cans. Prince and his band left the stage. They played one more show with the Stones, but that was the last show Prince played on that tour.

Prince was constantly writing new songs—so many that he started side projects for some of them. While he reserved the more rock- and pop-influenced songs for his own albums, he formed a band called the Time for his pure funk and R&B tunes. His old friend Morris Day, who had been the drummer in Grand Central with him back in high school, was the singer. Prince wrote all the songs and produced their self-titled album in his home in Chanhassen (near Minneapolis).

That fall Prince released his fourth album, *Controversy*. He had recorded it in nine days. As the title implied, the new album was designed to get people talking. Many fans had responded to *Dirty Mind* with all sorts of questions about Prince—what kind of music was he trying to make? Why did he dress that way? *Controversy* countered those questions with more questions—about race, sexuality, religion, and more—but very few answers.

Purple Rain

The next album was *1999*, and it changed everything for Prince. It contained even more focus on guitars and

rock-and-roll appeal than his earlier efforts, and it contained his biggest hits yet. "Little Red Corvette" reached the top ten in the United States and was his first song to do better on the pop chart than on the R&B chart.

The title track from *1999* was about the end of the

Prince plays his hit single "Little Red Corvette" on the television show *Solid Gold* in 1982.

world. When the album came out in 1982, the Cold War (1945–1991) between the United States and the Soviet Union (a former nation made up of fifteen republics, including Russia) was at a nerve-wracking peak. The two nations were stockpiling nuclear arms and seemed to be staring each other down, each waiting for the other to give in. In "1999" Prince imagines the moment of nuclear war.

While the idea of inevitable destruction might seem hopeless in the hands of another artist, Prince turned it into a party. His answer to the impending crisis was classic Prince: if the world is going to end anyway, we might as well dance and have fun now.

Prince's band in 1980, *from left*: bassist André Cymone, Prince, drummer Bobby Z. *(behind Prince)*, guitarist Dez Dickerson, and keyboardist Gayle Chapman

In the early 1980s, rocker Bob Seger regularly sold out huge venues, as he did at this show at Madison Square Garden.

Prince and his band, the Revolution, toured the United States to support *1999*, attracting the biggest crowds they had ever had. Still, while Prince was a huge cult hero back in Minneapolis, in other cities he was only a mid-level star. In fact, Prince noticed that the rock singer Bob Seger, who was touring many of the same towns at the same time as Prince, had a much bigger audience. Prince believed he was much better than Seger, and he asked Matt Fink why Seger had more fans.

Fink told Prince, "Well, he plays really straight ahead mainstream white rock and roll. If you created a song like that, you'd get even bigger."

Perhaps it was true that keeping one foot in his funk

and R&B roots prevented him from having a number 1 hit on the pop charts or selling out huge arenas as Bob Seger did. But already the band noticed that the crowds coming to their shows were changing. They were growing—and growing more white. Why? The answer, at least partly, was MTV.

At that time, Music Television was in its earliest days. The station had been criticized for playing almost no black artists. Two artists began to change that. One was Prince, whose video for "Little Red Corvette" was played regularly. The other was Michael Jackson, who released his masterpiece, *Thriller*, one month after *1999* came out.

Michael Jackson's *Thriller* album broke racial boundaries when it was released in 1982. As of 2016, it has sold more than one hundred million copies worldwide.

That album contained several massive hits, including "Billie Jean" and "Beat It," that were soon being played on MTV—a lot. Suddenly, Prince's vision of black and white music finding the same huge audience was becoming a reality.

Prince was still thinking about that "straight ahead mainstream" rock hit. He was also thinking about making a movie. In many ways, it was an outrageous idea. Prince may have had a big hit with *1999*, but did he really think he could get a major movie made? And that people would come to see it?

One band member, guitarist Dez Dickerson, didn't want to commit to a project that would take years of dedication. So he was replaced with Wendy Melvoin, who had been traveling with the group. Her girlfriend, Lisa Coleman, was already playing keyboards in the band. Wendy and Lisa became an iconic part of the Revolution and are often referred to with what sounds like a single word, "Wendy-and-Lisa."

Prince with bandmates Wendy Melvoin *(left)* and Lisa Coleman *(right)* in 1985

It was time for Prince to renew his contract with Warner Bros., but he told them the only way he would re-up was if they agreed to make his movie. Warner Bros. agreed to the deal.

A young director named Albert Magnoli worked on the script while Prince and his band worked on new songs for the movie. They played in a warehouse in the Minneapolis suburb of Saint Louis Park, where Prince ran intense, relentless practices. Susannah Melvoin, Wendy's sister, was hanging out with the band and growing close to Prince. "It was like the army," she said of practicing songs for the movie.

The movie would be loosely based on Prince's life, and a big part of it was his relationship with his parents. So while all the songwriting, practicing, acting lessons, script writing, and early production work was going on, Prince was also working to patch things up with his father. He visited his dad's home several times, and he invited his dad to practices.

Before filming began, Prince and the Revolution played a show at a nightclub called First Avenue in Minneapolis, where they debuted some of the new songs they'd been working on. The first encore was a song called "Purple Rain."

Wendy played the opening chords on a darkened stage. Soon Prince came out from the side and played some fills on his guitar. The rest of the band joined in, and Prince began to sing.

Magnoli approached Prince after the set and suggested that the song was powerful enough to be the centerpiece of the film. Prince claimed that they were still working on it, but he agreed that it was good. In fact, he asked Magnoli if they could title the movie *Purple Rain*. Magnoli agreed.

The story is about a character named the Kid (played by Prince), an up-and-coming musician in Minneapolis. At home, his violent father, a frustrated musician, is abusive toward his mother. A new girl, Apollonia, arrives in town, and she and the Kid begin a relationship. The Time is a rival band, and its leader, Morris Day, competes with the Kid for Apollonia's affection. The Kid's father shoots himself, but he survives the attempted suicide. The Kid sees that he has a lot in common with his dad, but he must avoid the darker temptations his dad succumbed to. Finally, he learns to give up some creative control in the band, which had been a source of conflict. That night he debuts a great new song written by other band members, he wins the girl, and he makes up with his dad.

In 1984 the album *Purple Rain* came out a month ahead of the movie. Reviews of the record were universally stellar. In a summer when the Jackson 5's Victory tour and Bruce Springsteen's *Born in the USA* got most of the headlines, the *New York Times* critic Robert Palmer wrote, "Long after this summer's hits are forgotten, and the Jacksons and Springsteen albums are packed away, *Purple Rain* will still be remembered, and played, as an enduring rock classic."

Reviews for the movie were less generous. The concert scenes, a big fraction of the film's running time, are terrific. But critics pointed out that the film as a whole is corny at times, and some of the acting is not very good.

Nevertheless, the movie was a hit in the box office, making more than $68 million. The album and the movie were smash hits with a wide audience, both black and white. *Purple Rain* finally transformed Prince into the megastar he always believed he would be.

The 1984 movie poster for *Purple Rain*

Fighting for Control

That fall the band launched a tour. But with Prince's new popularity, the tour was different from anything the band had experienced. When Prince and the Revolution came to town, they took over the city. Security locked down entire blocks, but still there was little privacy for band members. Tour manager Alan Leeds compared the over-the-top experience to tours put on by the Beatles and Rolling Stones. "It was the greatest show on earth," said Susannah Melvoin, who was not only in the Revolution but by this time was in a serious relationship with Prince.

Prince and sound engineer Susan Rogers were also busy recording new songs throughout the tour. The psychedelic *Around the World in a Day* was based on songs that Wendy and Lisa brought to him, though other members of the band

Prince plays guitar on the 1984 Purple Rain tour.

were less involved. In fact, Prince went back to his solo roots for this album, recording six of the nine songs on his own.

In 1985 *Purple Rain* was nominated for many awards. The sound track won two Grammys and one Oscar. Prince was also nominated for ten American Music Awards.

Prince could have made even more money on the Purple Rain tour if he had tried. He didn't tour outside of North America, and he cut off the tour after six months, while contemporary artists such as Bruce Springsteen toured for fifteen months worldwide. Prince was bored

In 1985 Prince worked with an architect to design a 55,000-square-foot home and recording studio. He named it Paisley Park, after the song on his album *Around the World in a Day*.

playing the same songs every night, and he became moody and grumpy.

With the sudden wealth he'd earned from *Purple Rain*, Prince built Paisley Park, a home and recording studio in the Minneapolis suburb of Chanhassen. Paisley Park also became the name of his own recording label, which was distributed by Warner Bros. and on which he released *Around the World in a Day*. Prince wanted to do something totally different from *Purple Rain* on the new record, and it was well received by critics. It sold more than two million copies, but fans didn't fall in love with it the way they did with *Purple Rain*.

Warner Bros. wanted another movie, and this time, Prince not only starred but also directed. But the movie was panned by critics and fans alike. *Under the Cherry Moon* was clumsy and unappealing. And it lacked the rock-and-roll appeal of *Purple Rain*.

To make matters worse, Prince and his girlfriend, Susannah Melvoin, broke up. They had fought before and broken up for short periods but had always gotten back together. But this time, it was done for good, and Prince was deeply hurt. His engineer and close friend Susan Rogers said that she saw a change in him that year. He began to act and dress differently, and he moped around Paisley Park.

Yet Prince's output never slowed. He had written and recorded so many songs, he presented Warner Bros. with a proposed triple album he called *Dream Factory*. He had

Prince in the Netherlands in 1986, on the Revolution's European tour

been working closely with Wendy and Lisa on the songs, and the two sang lead vocals on several of them. But Warner Bros. didn't want to release it. They argued that he was putting out music too quickly. *Around the World in a Day* was cutting into sales of *Purple Rain,* and if he released another album—especially a triple album—it would further damage sales of the earlier material.

Prince and the Revolution toured Europe and Japan, playing a funkier set than they had on the Purple Rain tour. In the shows, Prince played guitar less and danced more. And then, after the tour, Prince unexpectedly broke up the Revolution. Wendy, Lisa, and the others were devastated.

In 1987 Prince released *Sign o' the Times*, a double album cut down from the original triple album *Dream Factory*. Critics loved the record, and many fans and critics consider it to be the best record of his career.

But Prince's relationship with Warner Bros. had grown more difficult. They continued to argue over how quickly he should put out music. In 1993 Prince legally changed his name from Prince to a symbol that was a combination of the male and female symbols. It was his way of saying that the company might own his music, but it could not own him. The following year, Warner Bros. stopped distributing artists released by Prince's Paisley Park label. His final album for Warner Bros., *Chaos and Disorder*, was released in 1996. It was one of his least successful albums ever.

That year also was a low point for Prince personally. He married a dancer named Mayte Garcia, who became pregnant. Prince had a jungle gym built at Paisley Park in anticipation. But the child, named Boy Gregory, was born with Pfeiffer syndrome, a skull deformity, and he died after seven days on life support. A few years later, it was clear that Prince and Garcia could not recover from the devastation of losing a son together, and the two divorced.

Prince threw a release party for his 1997 *Emancipation* album to celebrate his freedom from Warner Bros.

Going It Alone

Finally free of Warner Bros., Prince recorded a triple album, *Emancipation*, and released it independently on his own label, the newly formed New Power Generation. In fact, he began releasing music on his label at an extraordinary rate. Though he didn't have much radio success during this period, his albums were critically well received.

They also sold well, due partly to Prince's experimenting with selling and marketing his music electronically, something mainstream record companies wouldn't figure out until many years later. He released a CD-ROM in 1994, *Prince Interactive*, that contained new songs, music videos, and an adventure computer game set at Paisley Park. In 1997 he sold his multidisc set *Crystal Ball* online.

Later, when technology companies, including music streaming services, began to grow, Prince would change his opinion of the benefits of the Internet. Online outlets didn't pay artists fairly, so Prince refused to allow any of his music to stream on Spotify or other services, and he vigilantly fought to remove unauthorized uses of his music on platforms like YouTube.

In 2001 Prince became a Jehovah's Witness. This conservative form of Christianity is similar to the Seventh-day Adventist Church that he grew up in. Like the SDAs, Witnesses believe that Jesus will come to Earth, judge everyone, and the world will end in apocalypse. Prince had always kept God and religious ideas in his music. In "Controversy," he recites the Lord's Prayer. In several songs, he conjures Judgment Day. Some people found it confusing that such a sexually explicit songwriter was religious. But Prince never believed that sex is a sin.

That same year, Prince got married again, this time to Manuela Testolini, an employee at his charitable foundation. He released his twenty-fourth album, *The Rainbow Children*. It contained even more apocalyptic imagery. In its review, *Rolling Stone* called Prince the "Freak-in-the-Pulpit." And Prince did get more conservative. In concert he stopped playing songs that he felt were too explicit. He even stopped swearing.

One requirement of being a Jehovah's Witness is that you have to talk to others about your religion. So Prince, just like all other Witnesses, went door to door and talked to people about salvation. He said people were often surprised to see Prince at their door. "But mostly they're really cool."

Of course, Prince continued to make music at an incredible rate. He often released albums without announcing or advertising them. But it is believed that most of the music he has produced has never been released. His former sound engineer, Susan Rogers, says she started keeping the tapes for everything he recorded in a big bank vault in Paisley Park. She said many songs, sometimes entire albums, went into the vault instead of being released. It's a practice Prince is said to have continued his whole life. Some fans and journalists have speculated that there is enough unreleased material to put out one album a year for a hundred years. Another recording engineer, Chuck Zwicky, said, "He was so prolific, by the time he released an album, he may have had

Prince at the 2007 Super Bowl halftime show

literally ten albums sitting around."

Besides producing new music, Prince continued to perform live. He had become known as one of the greatest live performers of all time. His performance at the 2007 Super Bowl is regarded as the game's best ever. He played a dramatic twelve-minute medley that included "Let's Go Crazy" and "Purple Rain"—all in pouring rain.

But a lifetime of dynamic performances was beginning to wear on Prince. He danced wildly and ran around the stage, playing many different instruments. He often did

acrobatic splits and jumps off of high speaker towers during shows. The impact of thousands of these moves—always while wearing high-heeled shoes—had begun to cause severe pain in his joints, especially his hips. Those who saw him later in his life noticed that he often limped.

At some point, he began to take powerful medication to fight the pain. Prince was famously clean all his life.

Prince announces the award for favorite soul/R&B album at the 2015 American Music Awards.

He didn't drink or do drugs, and he forbade his band members from doing them either. But he became addicted to the painkillers.

One night in April 2016, Prince was flying home to Minneapolis when he fell unconscious in the plane. The pilot made an emergency landing in Illinois, and first responders rushed to the scene. They were able to revive him from an overdose and save his life.

On April 20, Prince's representatives hired a doctor that specializes in drug addiction to come out to Paisley Park. Because the doctor was unable to come immediately, he sent his son on an overnight flight to be with Prince until he arrived. But when his son arrived at Paisley Park the next morning, he found Prince dead of an accidental overdose. He was lying alone in an elevator.

Though Prince was so often surrounded by fans, band members, and lovers, people said he was hard to get close to. As a child in a broken family, he learned not to trust anyone. As a brilliant teenager, he negotiated for—and got—a contract with a major record label that gave him complete control of and ownership over his music. He was always fiercely driven to produce more—and better—music, and this fire was something only he alone could tend to. So perhaps it is not surprising that he died alone, just as he always thought himself to be.

But he left behind an incredibly rich and vast catalog of music—and probably a lot more in the vault. For all the masterpieces Prince created, there are many more that we haven't even heard yet.

Important Dates

1958   Prince Rogers Nelson is born on June 7.

1965   Prince's parents separate.

1970   He begins living in his friend André's basement.

1976   He signs Owen Husney as his manager. With Husney's help, Prince signs a three-record deal with Warner Bros.

1978   Prince's first album, *For You*, is released on April 7.

1979   He and his band play their first live show on January 5. Warner Bros. decides not to have him tour. Warner Bros. releases his second album, *Prince*, in October.

1980   He plays on the TV show *American Bandstand*. He tours with Rick James. He releases his third album, *Dirty Mind*, to great reviews.

1981   He opens for the Rolling Stones and is booed off the stage.

1982   He releases *1999*.

1984   The album and movie *Purple Rain* make Prince a megastar.

1987   He releases the double album *Sign o' the Times*.

1993	After creative disputes with Warner Bros., Prince changes his name to a symbol and begins to be identified as "the artist formerly known as Prince."
1996	He marries dancer Mayte Garcia, and they have a son who dies at seven days old from a genetic skull condition.
2000	He and Garcia divorce. He changes his name back to Prince.
2001	He becomes a Jehovah's Witness and marries Manuela Testolini, an employee at his charitable foundation.
2004	He is inducted into the Rock & Roll Hall of Fame and plays the solo on George Harrison's "While My Guitar Gently Weeps."
2006	He and Testolini divorce.
2007	He performs the Super Bowl XLI halftime show.
2010	*Time* magazine names him one of the 100 most influential people in the world.
2016	He is treated for a drug overdose on April 15. He dies of an accidental drug overdose in his home at Paisley Park six days later.

SOURCE NOTES

10 Finn Cohen, "The Day Prince's Guitar Wept the Loudest," *New York Times*, April 28, 2016, http://mobile.nytimes.com/2016/04/28/arts/music/prince-guitar-rock-hall-of-fame.html.

14 "Oral History: Prince's Life, as Told by the People Who Knew Him Best," *Minneapolis Star Tribune*, April 29, 2016, http://www.startribune.com/the-life-of-prince-as-told-by-the-people-who-knew-him/376586581/#1.

16 Touré, *I Would Die 4 U: Why Prince Became an Icon* (New York: Atria Books, 2013), 27.

19 Ronin Ro, *Prince: Inside the Music and the Masks* (New York: St. Martin's, 2011), 25.

21 "Oral History," *Minneapolis Star Tribune.*

21 Michaelangelo Matos, "Do It All Night," in *The Genius of Prince* (New York: Condé Nast, 2016), 14.

22 "Oral History," *Minneapolis Star Tribune.*

26 Touré, *I Would Die*, 107.

29 Alan Light, *Let's Go Crazy: Prince and the Making of Purple Rain* (New York: Atria Books, 2014), 75.

31 Ibid., 168–169.

32 Ibid., 219.

38 Arion Berger, "Prince: The Rainbow Children," *Rolling Stone*, January 2, 2002, http://www.rollingstone.com/music/albumreviews/the-rainbow-children-20020102.

39 Claire Hoffman, "Prince's Life as a Jehovah's Witness: His Complicated and Ever-Evolving Faith," *Billboard*, April 28, 2016, http://www.billboard.com/articles/news/cover-story/7348538/prince-jehovahs-witness-life.

40 "Oral History," *Minneapolis Star Tribune.*

SELECTED BIBLIOGRAPHY

Azhar, Mobeen. "I Would Hide 4 You: What's Inside Prince's Secret Vault?" *Guardian* (US ed.), March 19, 2015. https://www.theguardian.com/music/2015/mar/19/i-would-hide-4-u-whats-in-princes-secret-vault.

Caramanica, Jon. "Prince, a Master of Playing Music and Distributing It." *New York Times*, April 22, 2016. http://www.nytimes.com/2016/04/23/arts/music/prince-music-technology-distribution.html.

Cohen, Finn. "The Day Prince's Guitar Wept the Loudest." *New York Times*, April 28, 2016.

Collins, Jon, Associated Press. "Autopsy: Prince Died of Fentanyl Opioid Overdose." *MPR News*, June 2, 2016. http://www.mprnews.org/story/2016/06/02/prince-cause-of-death.

Farber, Jim. "Kingdom of Sound." In *The Genius of Prince*. New York: Condé Nast, 2016.

Hoffman, Claire. "Prince's Life as a Jehovah's Witness: His Complicated and Ever-Evolving Faith." *Billboard*, April 28, 2016. http://www.billboard.com/articles/news/cover-story/7348538/prince-jehovahs-witness-life.

Holden, Stephen. "Prince: Controversy." *Rolling Stone*, January 21, 1982. http://www.rollingstone.com/music/albumreviews/controversy-19820121.

Light, Alan. *Let's Go Crazy: Prince and the Making of Purple Rain*. New York: Atria Books, 2014.

Matos, Michaelangelo. "Do It All Night." In *The Genius of Prince*. New York: Condé Nast, 2016.

Murray, Nick. "The Wisdom of Prince, as Told by His Collaborators." *New York Times*, April 27, 2016. http://www.nytimes.com/2016/04/28/arts/music/the-wisdom-of-prince-as-told-by-his-collaborators.html.

"Oral History: Prince's Life as Told by the People Who Knew Him Best." *Minneapolis Star Tribune*, April 29, 2016. http://www .startribune.com/the-life-of-prince-as-told-by-the-people-who-knew -him/376586581/#1.

Pareles, Jon. "Prince, an Artist Who Defied Genre, Is Dead at 57." *New York Times*, April 21, 2016. http://www.nytimes.com/2016/04/22/arts /music/prince-dead.html?_r=0.

Touré, *I Would Die 4 U: Why Prince Became an Icon.* New York: Atria Books, 2013.

FURTHER READING

BOOKS

Editors of Time. *Prince, an Artist's Life, 1958–2016.* New York: Time Books, 2016. This biography traces Prince's life story and career through fascinating stories from people who knew him.

Krohn, Katherine. *Michael Jackson: Ultimate Music Legend.* Minneapolis: Lerner Publications, 2010. Learn about Michael Jackson, an African American performer who rose in prominence around the same time as Prince.

Topix Media Lab editors. *Prince, 1958–2016. Newsweek* commemorative ed. New York: Topix Media Lab, 2016. Loaded with photos, this book looks back on Prince's life with a special focus on his influences and performances.

WEBSITES

"Prince," *Rolling Stone*
http://www.rollingstone.com/music/artists/prince
From this page, you can access every article about Prince in the influential rock magazine's archive.

"Prince, Tom Petty, Steve Winwood, Jeff Lynne, and Others: 'While My Guitar Gently Weeps'"
https://www.youtube.com/watch?v=6SFNW5F8K9Y
Watch the iconic performance of George Harrison's classic hit, and see Prince steal the show.

INDEX

Beatles, 8, 9, 32

Coleman, Lisa, 28, 32, 35, 36
controversies, 11, 22–24
crossover appeal, 8, 19–22, 24–28, 31

death, 11, 12–13, 41

family, 14–16, 29, 30, 36, 38, 41
Fink, Matt, 21, 22, 26

Garcia, Mayte, 36
Grand Central, 17, 23

Harrison, Dhani, 8–10
Harrison, George, 8–11

instruments, 7, 11, 12–13, 14–15,
    17–18, 19–20, 24, 28, 29, 40

Jackson, Michael, 27
Jehovah's Witnesses, 38–39

"Little Red Corvette," 24, 27

Magnoli, Albert, 29–30
Melvoin, Susannah, 29, 32, 34
Melvoin, Wendy, 28–29, 32, 35–36
MTV, 27–28

painkillers, 40–41
Paisley Park, 13, 33, 34, 36, 37, 39
Petty, Tom, 7, 10–11
pop music, 7, 12, 13, 19, 21–22, 23,
    24, 27
Purple Rain, 24–31, 33–35, 40

R&B, 13, 15, 19, 21, 23, 24, 26
recording, 11, 18, 19–20, 22, 24,
    32–33, 34, 37, 39
rock music, 7, 8, 11, 13, 15, 17, 19,
    21–23, 24, 26, 28, 31, 34
Rock & Roll Hall of Fame, 7–11, 13
Rogers, Susan, 32, 34, 39
Rolling Stones, 22–23, 32

school, 15–17, 23
Seventh-day Adventists (SDAs), 15, 38
Super Bowl performance, 39, 40

Testolini, Manuela, 38

Warner Bros., 18–19, 20, 34–36, 37
"While My Guitar Gently Weeps," 8–11